The *Perfect* Introduction: Detaching From my **Anger**

By A'Nesu Williams

Edited by Jhordynn of Made 4 This Publishing
(318) 406-2249

Cover designed by Psalmyy on Fiverr

Cover formatted by Psalmyy on Fiverr

Published by Made 4 This Publishing

ISBN-13 (paperback): 978-1-7365773-9-4

A Simple Prayer

Father, I pray in the precious name of Jesus for everyone who reads this book to feel your presence in the very moment of them reading it. I pray that yokes of bondage are broken off of their lives and the lives of their loved ones. I pray that the readers will be restored, that the blinders will be removed from their eyes, and that they become vulnerable with you, Father.

I pray that they allow You to heal their broken hearts and that they willingly walk into the process You've set before them to deliver them, set them free, and send them to the cities, states, regions, and nations that You've called them to! To minister the gospel!

I pray that the intercessor will arise in my brothers and sisters and that generational curses will be broken! I pray that someone decides to simply forgive! I pray that someone drops the heavy burdens they've been carrying for years and lets you have them!

I pray that every person who encounters this book experiences your love and your peace that surpasses all understanding! I pray that your overwhelming presence engulfs them in the name of Jesus! God, I pray that whatever each individual needs to receive from this book, they receive it by the power of the Holy Ghost! I pray that Holy Ghost Fire takes over each reader and never lets them go!

I pray that the anointing is ever so prevalent that everywhere they go, people see and announce the glory of God that rests even on their countenance.

In Jesus' name I pray. Amen.

Thank Yous

Father God, I want to thank you for sustaining my daddy, siblings, children, nieces, nephews, and everyone who was connected to and loved my mama. I want to thank you for calling me and springing me forth into my purpose for such a time as this. Thank you for your unwavering love and loyalty even when I have not been loving or loyal to You or the call. I'm forever surrendered to You!

Daddy, thank you for not giving up! You were with Mama all of y'all's lives! Fifty-five years together, fifty-three years of marriage done well! Thank you for always being the type of daddy that I could brag on. LOL. The type of daddy that all my friends loved growing up! Thank you for even taking on the role of Daddy to my sons whom you love with your whole heart and whom they love and inspire to be like. Thank you for holding it together for your family, even though you've had every reason to give up! And thank you for supporting and encouraging me to write! I love you, Daddy! Always have been and will always be my hero!

Thank you to my sons who stuck with me and covered me during the worst of these times when I had nothing to give to you three, not even myself. Your mom loves you beyond this life, and I appreciate all three of you!

To my Aunty Wanda, thank you for being a friend my mama could always depend on! Thank you for your continuous support and prayers through this entire time! Thank you for being my sounding board and voice of reason! Thank you for all the encouragement you gave through each chapter of this book. I really needed it. Thank you!

Pastor Nelson, thank you for keeping up with my daddy. We really appreciate your true and genuine friendship.

To my oldest brother, thank you for your support and permission! God has so much in store for you! This process wasn't easy for you. You suffered twice: losing Mama and having to nurse your son back to health. You're a lot like Daddy in your resilient silence, but you are a strong force! I love you, and I'm rooting for you always!

To my sister. Girl, with you and Mama being besties, I was really unsure of how this was going to work out! But you did it, and you're doing it!

I'm so Godly proud of the way you handled Mama's affairs and stuck right by Daddy's side through all the arrangements until the end. I'm not Mama, and I can't take her place, but consider me your new best friend until you and Mama reunite again. Then I guess I'll just go back to being your annoying little sister. Lol!

To my best friend Booska! Or Old Faithful as Daddy calls you! There aren't enough words in the dictionary to describe what type of sister friend you have always been! I love you to life! Thank you for always being by my side!

Dear Satan

Prince of Darkness, Beelzebub, Mephistopheles, Baphomet, Lord of the Flies, the Antichrist, Father of lies, Moloch, or simply Satan, just so it's clear that I'm talking to you, okay? I realize that you know who I am, but I would like to reintroduce myself. My name is A'nesu, which is of Zimbabwean origin, meaning "God is with us". I am also a prophet of the only wise and most high God!

You have been a nuisance my entire adult life. I even married your spawn at some point in my early twenties, and all except my brains were beaten out. But by the grace of God, I made it! I have been a single mother struggling to make it, even been homeless. The kids and I lived in a shelter, but by the grace of God, we made it!

I've had several heart breaks and disappointments! I've had those who claimed to love me turn on me just as Judas did Jesus with your influence. But… by the grace of God, I made it! I've done whatever I could to keep my head above water and to continue to love, even with a broken heart. I've done all that I've known how to keep it cool and mind my business.

I honestly just wanted a regular life for my kids and myself. But you, in the words of my late mother, "You just won't leave well enough alone now, would ya?" And speaking of my late mother, her name is Dorothy Faye Williams. I know you know that, too!

I just want you to know that I took the murder of my mama personal!!! And since war is what you want, then war is what you get!!!!! And this book is just a fraction of God's plan to reach God's people all over this world!!! To introduce them to our savior Jesus Christ! To walk them into deliverance! To show them it is possible to forgive the unfathomable! To usher them into God's miraculous healing power! To show them the way to stay connected to Christ!!!! To break generational curses! To cast out demons! To break yokes and chains of bondage!!! To break unGodly soul ties!!! To free us from strong holds! To expose the strong man and to dismantle your plans over the lives of God's people! To use this foul infraction you caused my family and me as an example to God's people that we are more than conquerors! And to be an example of how to use our weapon of worship as mass destruction to your ploys, plots, plans, schemes, and tricks! And to show God's people that every infraction should be used as the ladder to get us closer to God!

So, just in case you've misunderstood anything written above, let me lay it out for you: February 15, 2023, at 7:31pm, you declared war upon myself and my family.

Let the record show and state that this letter, my lifestyle of worship, repentance, and the acceptance of the call to carry this mantle is my response!

Luke 10:19- "I have given you authority to trample on snakes and scorpions and to overcome all the power of the enemy; nothing will harm you."

You ask if I'm mad. Of course not. I'm Holy Ghost fire pissed!

Signed,
Dorothy's Baby Girl and ~God's warrior~!

Chapter 1
February 15, 2023

Honestly, there's a part of me that wishes I never clicked over and answered the other incoming call, but I did, and now, I can't take it back! And I can't get my mama back!

"Hold on, Tesha. My sister is calling me on messenger," were the words I said to one of my best friends before my life was flipped upside down.

"Hello?" I asked, after I clicked over to my sister.

"Mimi!! Mimi!!" My sister was yelling my name. She sounded like she was crying and out of breath.

"Hey, Claire. Can you hear me?" I asked.

"Mimi, Mom was in a really bad car accident! I can't get to her! Sabrina and the boys are in the ambulance!"

I wish I could tell you what my mind was thinking in that moment, but I can't. All I remember is saying, "Wait. What?! Claire, where is my mama?!"

"Mimi, I don't know! I can't get to her. It was a bad wreck when I got here. I pulled up on the side of the ambulance. It's so many lights, I can't see. I just heard our nephew 4 crying, so I called out to him, and he answered. He was saying his legs are hurting!"

My sister was so upset. I knew it was bad! She was always the calm one. For her to be this unraveled, I knew it wasn't looking good. At this point, I was standing up in my room, looking around for something to put on quickly. I had just made it home from Bible Study, taken a shower, put on a cami, undies, and laid across the bed, waiting on my middle son to call me when he got off work. It was his first day on the job.

"Okay, 4's legs are hurting, but where is my mama?!"

"Mimi," she cried, "They won't let me get to her!"

"Okay. Where are y'all at?" I asked, as I grabbed a pair of sweats off of the clothes hamper that I had on earlier.

She told me where they were located.

"Okay! Here I come!"

I ran down the stairs of my townhome and headed for the front door. My youngest son must have heard the commotion, as our rooms were right across from one another.

He began running behind me. "Ma, what's going on? Where you going?!" he asked, but I was in too much of a hurry and didn't have enough information to tell him.

So, I said, "Use my bank card to get your brother a Lyft home at eleven pm. Don't forget him!"

I jumped in my car and sped off. I turned on my emergency flashers and hit eighty to ninety miles per hour in no time, passing up all stop signs and signals as cautiously as I could. Surprisingly, my friend Tesha was still on the line when my sister and I hung up, so I told her, "My mama been in a bad accident, and Claire talking about they won't let her get to my mama! So, I'm heading over there to see what's going on."

I don't remember Tesha's response or reaction. I just remember driving and pleading with God to not take my mama tonight and to please put my mama's soul back in her body. Once I got on I-20, my niece Angel called and said the family and everyone were headed to the hospital. I immediately detoured and headed to the hospital.

Once I arrived at the hospital, I jumped out of my car and began running to the emergency department. As I was running, I heard someone calling my name. "Mimi! Mi!"

I looked over my shoulder, and it was my first cousin Janeen running in the same direction as me. I ran into the emergency room, and I immediately saw my daddy sitting to the left of the waiting room.

"Hey, Daddy. Where's my mama?" I asked him.

He looked at me with so much concern in his eyes and said, "I don't know, Baby. They asked us to wait here."

That was not a good enough answer for me, so I walked over to the front desk and spoke to an older Caucasian worker who was sitting behind it. I assumed she was a nurse or a desk clerk. I didn't know, and I didn't care. I needed answers *NOW!*

"Hi, there. My mother was just involved in a horrible car accident. Can you tell me where they have her at?"

The Caucasian woman looked at me without ever touching her computer and said, "Oh, no, I wouldn't know."

So, I leaned over the desk and gave her my mother's name and date of birth. "Ma'am, my mother's name is Dorothy Williams. Her birthday is May 22, 1955. Can you put that in your computer?"

She replied, "There's been three major car accidents tonight, and they are all coming in at the same time. The doctor is the only one who can tell you about your mother. I cannot."

"Well, then get me a doctor! Please!"

I was just about losing my cool, or acting like my mama, as my daddy would say. My mama was always sure to get the business straight!

There were two other front desk clerks: two African American women who walked over to my daddy and was speaking to him. One looked to be comforting him as she laid her hand on his shoulder, so I walked over toward Daddy, hoping they were giving him some information about my mama. But they didn't have any, either. They were just offering words of comfort.

Things were happening so fast! At some point, both of my older brothers showed up. One whose youngest child and only son was in the car with our mama. We affectionately called my brother's son— my nephew— 4 because he is the fourth, named after my brother, father, and grandfather. My other brother's youngest daughter and grandson—they were mother and son, Sabrina and Tay— were both in the car with Mama as well. 4 was rushed into emergency surgery, and Sabrina and her baby were being seen. My oldest brother was taken to the ICU with his son while the rest of us were waiting to find out where Mama was.

My brother received a call from his kids' mother who had stayed at the crime scene with my mom while everyone else had come to the hospital. When he answered the phone, I was waiting for him to say something, but instead he was just saying, "Uh huh, wait, what?" His face went flushed, and he walked off, so I decided I was going to find my own mama!

I left the hospital, ran to the parking lot, jumped in my car, and headed back to the interstate toward the direction of the crash site. As I was getting onto I-20, it began to drizzle, and I thought, "No, God, not the rain! I gotta get to my mama!"

And in that instant, the Holy Spirit spoke back saying, "Go back to the hospital with your family; you all are going to need one another." So, at the next exit, which was about a mile from where I got on at, I got off and took the streets back to the hospital. It was confirmed in my spirit that my mother was gone.

I drove silently back to the hospital. No music, no conversation on the phone, just pure silence. I don't remember having any thoughts, neither do I remember stopping at any red lights or slowing down at any yellow lights. But as I am reliving the night of February 15, 2023, in my mind, I can still see switching from yellow to red. What's funny is I never see green lights when I replay the moments back in my mind.

I pulled back up to the hospital, parked, and got out my car. Everything in that moment seemed to be moving in slow motion. I don't know. Perhaps it was me moving in slow motion.

I began walking back towards the emergency department. Outside, I spotted the two African American front desk clerks as they spotted me, but I didn't say anything to them. I believe I was too heartbroken and in a state of pure shock! When one of the ladies said, "Hey, Sweetheart, did you all find your mom?" I responded, "No, she's dead."

"Oh, my goodness! I mean, did they tell you that?"

I shook my head no and shrugged my shoulders.

Then one of the sweet ladies said, "Well, can I give you a hug and pray with you?"

I nodded my head yes, so they both embraced me and began praying for me in the parking lot, and suddenly my legs were growing weak, and the ugliest scream came up from my wounded soul. "NOOOOOOOOOOOOOOOO, GOOOOODDDDDDD!!!!!! NOT MY MOMMMMMAAAAA!!!! THEY KILLED MY MAMA!!!!!" I dropped to my knees on the gravel in the parking lot.

The ladies grabbed me by either arm and began trying to help me back to the seat of my car. They were able to get the car door open, but I slid to the ground on my knees again. I know what my posture is when I need God's attention!

Those sweet ladies were praying and trying to get me up when I heard my oldest brother saying, "Mimi, Mimi. Come on, Mimi. We don't know, yet."

But the truth was I knew my mama was gone, and my heart was shattered. I was inconsolable. I was sobbing profusely when I heard another sweet, manly voice. My oldest son Markel said, "Mom, Mom, come on, Mom. What's going on?"

Apparently, someone contacted him while he was at work and told him to get to the hospital, but they didn't fill him in on what was going on. I was finally able to get in my car, but I just couldn't stop crying. Finally, my daddy walked up. Those same two hospital clerks were offering their condolences to Daddy, but he was more concerned about making sure his kids were okay. He was trying to head back to the scene where my mother was, but my oldest brother, my son, and nieces wouldn't allow Daddy to leave alone.

Once I gathered myself, I noticed that my family was outside in the parking lot with me. I'm not sure how they knew I was out there, but I was so glad that they were. I needed every last one of them. I got out my car to walk across the street to the emergency department with the rest of my family when I began to hear the screams of my nieces and my oldest son. I looked across the street, and I could see my sister coming around the back side of the emergency department holding her chest, saying, "Lord, no, please. Not my mama!"

My nieces dropped to the ground, screaming out loudly. My oldest son was crying so hard. I hadn't heard him cry like that since he was a little boy. I walked across the street to all of my family who had just gotten the news and began trying to help console them. I felt weak and faint, but my son needed me now. My niece and sister were so bent out of shape. We were trying to grab a hold of the other small great grand kids. It was a living nightmare!

It had been confirmed: my mama was dead. The only information that we had at the moment was a drunk driver was responsible. I don't know who confirmed it. It didn't even matter. My mama was gone.

As everyone was still crying out and cursing, screaming to the top of their lungs, I walked my son to the steps of the emergency department, sat him down, and walked away from everyone. I went and sat on the concrete of the ramp to the main entrance of the hospital. I could still hear the cries, and although they were close, they sounded as if they were in the distance. It was eerily quiet with distant cries, screams, and whimpers, all while so still and silent. I just sat. I don't remember having any thoughts whatsoever. I just sat there.

Suddenly, a small, still voice, the voice of God asked me, “Do you still love me?”

Without hesitation, I said, “Yeah.”

Then he said, “Do you still trust me?”

And I said, “Yes.”

Then there was silence.

While sitting there after my encounter with God, anxiety crept in. I hurried and got up from where I was sitting for fear that someone may be drunk driving and will ride down off the road and kill me.

Chapter 2
"The Final Visit"

"Hey, Guh!" I greeted my mother as we always did to one another playfully, using our southern not-so-southern accents.

Now having lived in the south for almost twenty years, one may think we would sound southern, but whenever we spoke to southerners, they would immediately notice that we weren't from around there. Well, in my mother's case, she was from Shreveport, Louisiana, but had lived, bore her children, and raised us in Long Beach, California, so she did not have the accent, either.

"Hey, Nesa!" she affectionately called me at times.

I walked in the door of my parents' home and followed my mother to the den where she and my two nephews were hanging out.

"Mama, look!" I said, pointing to the seat of my pants.

We both burst out in laughter.

"Gurrrrlllll!! "Why is all your tail hanging out the crack of your pants like that?!"

We laughed even more.

"Guhhhh! When I was climbing over the fire wall at work, I got snagged and ripped my pants, Guh! Good thing I have on tights under these jeans, huh?!"

We laughed a good minute about it, then I asked her if she had any sweats I could fit because it was Wednesday night, and I had Bible study to attend to. She didn't have any. She said I had taken them all and not returned them, which was true. As she said that, I remembered that I had a pair of sweats in my trunk, so I ran back outside to my car to get them.

Once I came back inside the house, she said, "Oh, here, Nessarah (which was another nick name she sometimes called me. Short, not so short, for Anesu). Get your card before I forget to give it back to you."

A day or two prior, I had given her my debit card and allowed her to do some grocery shopping, so she was giving it back to me.

"Mama," I said, "you ain't cooked nothing? I don't smell no hog maws or chitlins. No nothing!"

She wouldn't really be making hog maws or chitlins. That was just me joking, but seriously asking her about dinner. My mother and father had been together roughly fifty-five years and would have made fifty-three years of marriage had she not passed. She cooked almost every day in honor of him and out of the pleasure of being his wife. So, I stopped by daily in the morning before I headed to the yard and in the evenings when I got off work. The yard is what we called the place where truck drivers go to pick up their trucks for their shifts. Most evenings, I could sit and eat and pack my sons some dinner to carry home with me.

"Nah, Girl. I had the kids today and ran to the store. But by the time I got back here, not too long before you just pulled up, I knew I wouldn't have time to cook before going to pick up Brea from work. But I'll figure something out for your daddy once I get back home."

I was disappointed because that meant after church I had to figure something out for me and my two youngest sons who still lived at home with me. But I just said, "Okay."

I picked her sales papers up off the side of her on the couch. As she put them down, we talked about sales, and she had asked about the new guy I had met and was talking to. I was telling her that I didn't think I was going to keep him around, and she asked me why.

Right when I opened my mouth to explain, she said, "He must put his pants on one leg after the other?" This was her way of saying that I found something wrong with every man.

We fell out laughing!

I said, "Um, no, Ma'am. He seems to be a liar!"

I was telling her that I thought it was awfully strange that his first ex-wife sent him a Happy Valentine's Day card. I told her that it seemed like what he wasn't saying was since the second ex-wife left him, he dipped back to the first one, and I was not about to be going through all of that with these people! I had just turned forty-one a month prior, and I had no interest in being in competition.

My mother looked up from her sales paper and said, "Nesu, did he not just help you pay for your lawyer?"

I said, "Yes."

"Did he just introduce you to his family and have you at his daughter's party?"

"Yes."

"Is the ex-wife asking him why she wasn't invited?"

"Yes."

She said, "Sounds like there is no competition, Baby. She doesn't want him no way, I guarantee you. He makes more money now than he did when she was with him, and she's just trying to get a piece of the pie."

Lol. My mama always had a way with words. She would make you think long and hard about things. She came from the old school where men probably got away with a lot more than I am willing to allow someone to get away with on me simply because I've been through it and don't like the way it makes me feel. But my mother was the type of woman that if she wanted it, she got it; if she didn't want you to have it, you weren't getting it, or it was going to be a hell of a fight! I admired that about her in a sense.

Shortly after our conversation, the guy I had been talking to her about called. She had never met him before. Since he called on FaceTime, I let them meet.

"Mom, this is D'angelo. D, this is my mama, Mrs. Dorothy."

She looked up in the phone and smiled at him and waved. "Hey there."

He smiled back. "Hey there, Mrs. Dorothy. Nice to finally meet you."

"Yes, indeed. You, too!"

I quickly ended the call with him because I was still unsure about the relationship and didn't want them talking too much. Lol. When I hung up, I remembered that I had forgotten to pack her Valentine's Day chocolate Turtles to bring to her. I told her I would bring them to her tomorrow. I was rushing off to church. I had stayed over talking too long and was running late. I told her I would see her tomorrow. We both told each other, "See you later," but neither of us knew that later wasn't ever coming. Well, at least not on this side of heaven.

I left my parents' house and went straight to Bible study. I remember Bible study let out early because our pastors had taken a little vacation, so an associate minister brought the lesson that night. When I left the church, I called my mama to ask her if she had spent the amount we discussed on my debit card, and she said she did. As a matter of fact, she spent a little less than we agreed. I said, "Okay, then," and we hung up the phone. That would be the last time I would hear my mother's voice ever!

A few hours later, my sister called me. She told me that my mom was in a car accident. Just like that, Mama was gone.

Chapter 3
Day 2

I was able to only sleep for two hours once I actually could rest my mind enough to lay down. I'm still not sure how I got my mind to slow down. Had to have been God. Only He can give you the peace that passes all understanding and unexplainable rest. "My mama just died" and "sleep" don't belong in the same scenario, unless God has something to do with it. Two hours isn't much, but it was better than zero hours. That was two more hours than I expected to get.

I woke up to the sun shining bright through my window and reality gut-punching me. It had been eleven hours since my mother had crossed over into glory. I was riddled with sorrow. I sat straight up in my bed and just started crying again. I just remember praying through my tears, "God, please, you gotta help us. I don't know what to do, but I know You do."

Court for a prior incident I was involved in was in a couple hours. My best friends Thomas and Yolanda had asked me the night before if I was going to call my lawyer and reschedule, but I refused. I was more ready than ever before to confront the Caucasian teens who ran into the back of my eighteen-wheeler work truck and their parents who did not hold them accountable. My mother dying at the hands of an immature, irresponsible driver gave me the fuel I needed to go to court and let my voice be heard regarding those teens and their actions.

August 13th, 2022, at approximately 11:00 pm, I was exiting a battery tank location on a dark road in south Helen. As I was completing a left turn, some teens came speeding out of nowhere and crashed into the driver side of my trailer, busting the rear tire, damaging the toolbox, and totaling out their vehicle.

In the south, as much as I was holding out hope that racism wasn't as prevalent as I had heard, I unfortunately had the opportunity to experience it firsthand. All these Caucasian firefighters showed up questioning me and trying to get my information. That was confusing to me because although I had never been in an accident before of any kind, I knew enough to know that the police are the ones who are supposed to show up and ask for your driver's license and insurance.

But everything was put into perspective later when I found out the teen was training with the fire department, and his father was some big shot in the area. So needless to say, they tried to pin the at-fault on me! And there was no way I was going to reschedule my court date. I was more than ready to share my mother's story of being killed by a negligent driver to the kids who hit my truck and their parents who were trying to cover for them. I was more than ready to explain how those parents not holding their son accountable will one day result in him killing someone or himself.

Before arriving at court, I had called my lawyer's office and had spoken with her receptionist to let her know what had transpired with my mother the night before. I asked her if she could make me her first client of the day so that I didn't have to sit in court for hours waiting to be seen. I'm assuming she agreed to this because she showed up early.

When I arrived at court, my two besties Yolanda and Thomas were already there waiting in the hallway outside the court room. They both greeted me with a hug and told me that the bailiff had told everyone that if they were just there for support, they would have to stay outside in the hallway because there weren't enough seats inside of the court room. I proceeded to walk inside the court room and take a seat.

About ten minutes after sitting, my lawyer walked in, went to the front, spoke with a few people, the opposing lawyer, and the clerk. She was able to get me called up to the front to speak with the judge. I was given a new court date to return two months later to continue with the trial.

Once I left the courtroom, both Yolanda and Thomas walked me out to my car and assured me that they were with me every step of the way. They told me to give them a call whenever I needed them. When we departed from one another, I got into my car and began crying again. Tears just began to flow down my face. The weight of my mama being gone just seemed like it was too much to bear.

I remember glancing up toward heaven and asking, "What do I do, Mama? I don't know what to do."

Then a thought popped up in my mind. I knew that if my mama had made it, she would have been at the bedside of both my nephews who were injured in the car wreck with her. So, that was my answer, to go check on my nephews. I couldn't be Mama, and I never will be, but I could at least try to be who she was to my family. I could at least try to take the edge off of the void that they were feeling.

I went to my daddy's house. I let him know I was okay, and that court was pushed back. I knew to check on my daddy and my sons who were there with him. I specially made sure to check on my oldest son who had passed out the night before.

Once I got to Daddy's house, I told him that I was going to head up to the hospital to go and check on 4 and my nephew Tay. Before I left, he handed me a bag of items for 4, which included his favorite candy, a few Cokes, and his favorite pajamas. I left Daddy and headed to the hospital, the whole time dreading what I would see, feel, hear. I prayed some more and gave myself pep talks.

My niece Sabrina and her son Baby D, who were both in the accident with Mom, were still in the downstairs emergency department room, so I went to see them first. They were still being seen for their injuries. As I walked up on the room, there were two young ladies I hadn't met before, who were my niece's friends. They greeted me with a hug and gave me their names, which I cannot recall at this time.

I walked into the hospital room my niece was in. My niece was laying in the hospital bed, and her son's grandmother was holding my niece's son. He was wearing only a diaper. He had superficial scratches on his little body, but his lungs were bruised and swollen with fluid. He was crying profusely, even in his sleep. Both Ralph and Sheila— Tay's grandparents— greeted me and gave their condolences. I thanked them and began to cry again.

I told Sabrina that I was going upstairs to check on 4 and my oldest brother, and then I would be back. When I walked out the room, the young ladies who were waiting to see Sabrina asked me, "How are you?"

Now, I know I was so numb. I had never felt that feeling before, so when they asked how I was doing, I had to think about it. The only thing I could answer with was, "I don't know. I've never lost my mama before."

One of the young ladies hugged me again, and she said, "I know the pain. My mama died a few years ago, and it's been crazy, but we making it. You gone be alright."

I turned and proceeded up the hallway to the elevator to check on my brother, eldest brother, and his son 4.

I tried hard to suck it up and prepare myself for what I was about to see. I didn't know if my nephew's face would be messed up, or if my brother would be emotional. All I knew was that I wanted to be strong for them. After all, my nephew didn't call my mama Grandma; he called her Mama.

My brother didn't just lose his mama, but he almost lost his only son. And although his son pulled through, he had physical injuries most seven-year-olds would never experience and emotional scars that will probably haunt him for the rest of his life! Surely, I didn't want to add to it, so I got myself together as best as I could.

I opened the door to 4's room. "Hey, Y'all," I spoke.

My poor nephew spoke back in such a small voice engulfed with pain. I wasn't sure if the sound of his voice was from physical pain, medication induced fatigue, or if my brother had told him that Mama was gone.

I asked him, "Are you hurting, 4?"

He said, "No, TT. It's just that my mama was in the car accident."

Cutting him off, I said, "Oh, yeah, I know, but Grandpa sent you some snacks!" I said, while raising his favorite candy up out the bag along with his Cokes.

He gave me a little smile, and I felt a sense of relief.

My brother's demeanor was real cool; he had no expression. So, I stepped behind my nephew to where he couldn't see me. I mouthed to my brother, "Did you tell him about Mom?"

To my surprise, my brother said, "Yeah, he knows. As soon as his eyes opened this morning, he looked at me and said, 'Daddy, is my mama dead?' And I just told him the truth."

When I heard my brother say those words, I promise it took everything in me to not scream and holler! But I held it together. 4 began to ask if he could eat some of his candy and drink his soda that his papa sent him. I asked his nurse, but she said he couldn't because they had him on some type of diet and would send him some fruit to his room within the hour. I relayed the message to my brother, and then I left shortly, heading back down to Sabrina and Baby Tay's room.

As soon as I opened her room door, she asked me how 4 was doing. I told her he was lying there with cartoons on; not much he could do. She asked if he knew about Mama. When I told her he did, we both just broke down and started crying. It hadn't been a whole twenty-four hours since Mom had gone to glory, and it was getting more and more difficult by the minute.

I left the hospital and went back to Daddy's house. When I pulled up, there were so many cars there! Immediate feelings of being overwhelmed and gratitude fell upon me. I was happy that so many people loved my mama and were showing my daddy and the rest of us love; but I was so overwhelmed by people who were showing up, talking too much, asking a million questions.

The number of calls that were coming in with people falling out over the phone crying harder than us was entirely too much! But I understood. I just wished they understood how much worse they were making it on the family. However, I've been guilty of some of the same offenses because you honestly don't know until you've gone through it.

I wished my mama could have seen who all came through and brought flowers. Oh, man, she would have been through the roof! She loved plants and flowers. I also wished she could see who all came to support Daddy, near and far.

But most of all, I wished she could see the ones she treated like she birthed who never came! Not to the house, to the funeral, nothing! The same people she had loved! The same ones she made a big deal out of their homecoming whenever they would come into town, cooking them the finest of steaks with loaded potatoes and delicious gourmet salads, or fried catfish, okra, corn and tomato, homemade mac n cheese, jambalaya, dirty rice, or her famous gumbo!

My mother was an amazing cook, and cooking was a part of her love language. She loved these people, and they proved, in my opinion, not to love her back! One of them had stopped being my favorite long ago when Mama was living. Just too bad Mama couldn't see what the heck I was talking about.

Anyway, we absolutely enjoyed and appreciated those who did show up, sent cards, kind words of encouragement, prayers.

Chapter 4
Dorothy Faye Williams

My mama was a real riot! Here are some memories of her in no particular order. Just a few moments to share with you all as a glimpse to all of her many character traits.

My mama's obituary was pretty good at summing up the basics about who she was. I still have a hard time talking about her in past tense, but I digress. My sister Claire did a phenomenal job writing the obituary. However, I would like to take this opportunity to expound on the life well lived by Dorothy Faye.

My mama was a force to be reckoned with! Lol! You had better believe it! She meant business! She tolerated no disrespect from anyone! You weren't going to play with her husband, her children, her money, and you'd mess around and lose your life when it came to her grand and great grandchildren. She was a fierce protector. She always stood her ground and yours, too! Lol.

She was an elite businesswoman! She was stern while we were children! She took "I ain't one of your little friends" to a whole different level! You respected her and other adults, or you paid gravely for it!

My daddy worked away from home all my childhood life, so she was basically raising the five of us who were in the home by herself. With nooo problem! Trust me. She had it all under control! Her way or no way! She played no games!

She believed heavily in disciplinary actions; she had a belt named Lucy. Lucy was a thick black utility belt (now worn out). I can't remember what job she held before I was born, but Lucy was a part of her uniform and became my mom's disciplinary side kick. The two of them together meant business! My mom with Lucy was like dual super butt kicking power!

I was afraid of my mom and Lucy when came time for butt whippings! Even our friends were afraid of Lucy! My mom and Lucy did not discriminate. If you came to her house and cut up, you'd meet Lucy. My "fast friends", as Mama called them, did not like to spend the night with me.

Although extremely strict, my mama was also hard working. She was the epitome of a hustler! I get my hustle from her. She owned a few businesses, she catered, ran a twenty-four-hour childcare, she even had a boutique at one time just to name a few.

She could be really nurturing, too! She took in and cared for her Uncle Joseph who had been bedridden since before I was born, which completely rearranged our entire lives. She went out of her way to help those in need. When my grandfather took sick, she also took care of him until he passed away from cancer.

She, in one way or another, helped all her children raise her grandchildren. She enjoyed having them around and often would attempt to overrule our parenting authority. She crunched toes often and made no apologies for it.

My mama was a bit of a control freak. She felt like everything should go her way, and she had a very peculiar way of seeing to things aligning the way she felt they should happen. Her way or the highway lol.

Dorothy Faye loved attention, although she always claimed she didn't. Lol. My mom was extremely competitive. One of my male siblings is just like her, but I won't say any names. She hated to lose, and anything not going her way felt like a loss to her.

Mama was an astounding cook! Nobody, and I do mean nobody, could fry catfish like her. Oh, and her mac and cheese is still unmatched. Your great granny couldn't touch her dressing with an angel's fingertip, and she knew it!

She had an aura about her that said, "Anything you could do, she could do better." Lol. I laugh because it was annoying, and I couldn't tell you for the life of me where she got that from. But it was her, and no matter who tried to tell her about herself, it went in one ear and out the other. No one could put my mama in her place! If you tried it, you were just walking into the ring with a mighty force and would be sure to regret your decision once she was finished giving you a piece of her mind! She was theee uncheckable!

Although my mama was tough as nails, she still had a soft spot for my daddy, her husband of fifty-three years! She loved to tell the story of how she first laid eyes on him while she was a little girl on the school yard and my daddy was passing by. She didn't know it at the time, but her best friend was one of his younger sisters.

She told her best friend (Daddy's younger sister), "Oh, he's going to be my husband."

Her friend said, "Who? Brother?"

Mama said she was like, "That's your brother?!"

Needless to say, she started hanging around her best friend's house more often. Mama loved to brag about the fact that Daddy was supposed to be marrying someone else who was closer to his age. This woman was also a very pretty woman with a good job, but Mama said she always knew Daddy was her man! Lol.

My daddy's older sister Aunt Maxine once told us, "Dorothy would go home late that evening, and early the next morning, you would see her coming right back down the hill to our house." My mama was the epitome of "My man, my man, my man." Lol.

I would show her a guy I was talking to, and she would say, "Yeah. He's alright, I guess. He ain't none of your daddy." Or, "He ain't as handsome as my honey! But he'll do."

One time, my sister Claire, Mama, and I were in the kitchen at Mama's house, and I showed her this guy. Mama looked at his picture and said, "Mmm hmm… yeah, he's ugly enough!"

My sister said, "Mama, he ain't ugly! Mama don't think nobody looks good but that old Black man in the room back there!"

Mama told Claire, with her middle finger extended, "You got damn right! And you go straight to hell, you hear!"

Lol!!! My mama was hilarious! Anytime I would talk highly of someone I was dating, she would say, "Oh, you see what my man got me, huh? Tell ya man to step his game up!"

Mama loved to dote on her husband!

My mother wasn't afraid of anything or anyone! When I was just a little girl, we were rolling down the streets of the east side of Long Beach. We got to the stop sign near Hill and Louis.

There was a man in a Sanford and Son truck in front of us. The man was sitting at the stop sign not moving, so Mama honked the horn at him. The man hung his head out the window, cursing Mama out, so she started cursing back at him!

The man jumped out his truck. I was so petrified! This guy was a wide back, big belly, tall, Black man with a long beard! Do you think Mama cared?! Well, you're awfully wrong if you think she did!

I started crying. "Mama, goooo!" I begged her to drive off and leave the man in the dust.

Dorothy threw that car in reverse and told that man, "I'll run your ass over!"

He hurried to jump back in his truck. "Crazy woman!" he said, as he sped off!

Then Mama turned to me and said, "Shut your mouth! You don't do no crying while I'm fighting, hell!"

Mama stood about 5'3", but you would have thought she was six feet in stature with a degree in body building the way she stood up to any and everyone!

Dorothy loved to say, "I'm not cooking this time!" only to cook anyway because she didn't know if people's homes were clean enough to eat out of. Ha ha ha! She would say she was going to let someone else at the church cook because "I'm tired, hell! Now me and Ole Dale," who was her pastor, "gone have to talk about all this here because I had to cook for the Women's Retreat and Father's Day luncheon. You know I don't mind, but I mean, hell!"

We just listened to her because well, we knew she'd be in the streets dragging Claire along, going from store to store buying up everything needed in order to decorate nicely and cook the best food Shreveport had tasted since Buck was a pup, and now he was a grown ass dog! (In her words.) My mama had some sayings that would send you clean up under a table in laughter! She would offend people often, but people also loved her!

For years, she never really gave me any relationship advice. But I would often have people tell me, "You know I ran into your mother the other day, and I was really down about my marriage, just ready to throw in the towel. But she encouraged me in such way I decided not to file for divorce." Or, "You know, Mrs. Dorothy told me to come by and get her famous chef salad for my job's potluck." And, "Oh, Baby, you know I wouldn't have anyone else keep my kids! Grandma Dorothy is right where all my kids will be at!"

My mother had a love for children. All her daycare kids honestly thought she was their grandma. Parents would often come in the door expecting a warm embrace from their kids, only for them to sit on Mama's lap, looking at their parents like, "What are you doing here?"

In other cases, the children would be excited to see their parents but wouldn't leave without thoroughly loving on Mama! If you brought your baby to her, she was rocking them, teaching them to pray, as well as teaching them their ABCs, singing with them, dancing with them, and most definitely feeding them! Oh, and not to forget to mention, she nursed them right on back to health when they were sick!

Mama hated funerals, but she empathized with people who suffered loss. So, she would cook for the grieved families, stop by their loved one's homes after, and take plants. She would even attend the funerals to show her respect.

If my mama loved you, you knew it! Because she was sure to protect you! She was ready to go to war behind anyone, if that meant telling you how to fight legally, or giving you advice on what to say to defend yourself; if that meant showing up to defend you or whatever the means were, she was coming through!

If you were ever blessed to meet my mama, you'd never forget the experience. Whether she was praying for you, making you laugh, disciplining you, checking you, encouraging you, cooking, or feeding you, you wouldn't forget her. There will never be another Dorothy Faye Williams.

My mama and I had a very interesting relationship. In fact, her relationship with each of her children was different, and it's probably because we all have different personalities. But she and I did not always get along. I didn't always agree with her way of thinking, her way of doing things, or a lot of things she would say. I'd tell her my opinions or my thoughts that were opposite of hers, and of course, that didn't blow over well. Sometimes, it would lead to full blown arguments; other times, it would lead to her putting me out of her house or simply hanging up in my face.

She never apologized for anything. Well, at least not to me. And having known her my whole life, I honestly stopped looking for her to so many years ago. The truth is we had our own type of relationship, and it was far from perfect! However, it didn't stop us from loving one another.

As a matter of fact, about six months or so prior to her passing, I was in prayer. I was reminding God that in 2011 He sent a prophet who did not know my mother or myself to tell me that God was going to fix our relationship. I asked him when. In that moment, I was prompted by the Holy Spirit to first apologize for whatever I had done to my mama to make her feel the way she did towards me. The Holy Spirit also prompted me to let her know that I forgave her for everything I felt she had done to me.

I did, and of course, she didn't reciprocate an apology. But she did accept mine, and she told me she loved me. So, from that day, I started going to my parents' house almost every morning before work and every evening after work. This was to establish a better relationship with her. I accepted that she was just Dorothy, and I had only one mama. I could spend the rest of our days being bitter, or I could spend the rest of our days doing things that made us better. For me, making things better was seeing her every day on purpose.

Daddy would take my muddy oilfield uniforms and wash them while Mama typically had cooked dinner. That would be our time to chat about any and everything. I would be telling her about that bad baby of hers, who is my youngest son Dayton. He was seventeen at the time, trying to find his way into "The School of Hard Knocks". She refused to believe he was being a complete knuckle head!

I would bounce ideas off of her. She and I were a lot alike in the sense of serial entrepreneurship endeavors. We definitely wouldn't let anything, or anyone, stand in the way of what we desired for our lives.

She and Daddy didn't think it was a good idea for me to become a truck driver. But I thought it was a great idea, and I knew God had brought the opportunity back around, so I jumped on it! They were both proud! Whenever I would come in after work, she would say, "Cash app me fifty dollars," on Monday. And by Friday, it was, "Cash app me one hundred dollars." Lol. Not because she needed it, but because I had made the mistake of telling her how much I was making in a week.

Mama was definitely the queen of spending your money! Lol! She would call me on my days off, especially if I told her I was going to grab the boys or me some shoes or clothing items. She was sure to call me with her order. The funniest would be her text messages, "Hello Nesu this is mom."

Ha ha ha! Oh my gosh, it would be so funny! I would reply, "Mama I know it's you! I have your number programmed in my phone!"

Laughing hysterically through texts, she would text back, "Well hell call me!"

When I would call, she would say, "What y'all over there doing?"

She was hoping I would say that we had made it to the mall so that she could turn my short shopping trip into a whole day of shopping for her, which was so annoying. If Mama sent you to the store or learned you were in the store, and she started putting in requests, you were staying longer than you had anticipated. Any other plans you had for the day were being put off! Lol.

My mama respected my taste in clothes and accessories, so when she was murdered, it was only right for me to buy her clothes, accessories, have her hair done professionally by my best friend Yolanda, and do her make-up myself.

My daddy loved to purchase and see Mama dressed in the finest of clothes So, instead of going to our chick stores where the discounts were plentiful, I went to Dillard's in Pierre Bossier Mall. Daddy loved to see Mama in white and insisted that she wear white for her homegoing celebration. So, I found her a beautiful two-piece white skirt and jacket (blazer) with the all-white blouse that went underneath.

Her nails were already freshly done. She would normally wear garnet red on her nails, but this time, she had a nice clear coat on her nails. Mama loved pearls, so I was sure to get her a nice pearl necklace with pearl earrings and a dainty pearl bracelet. The mortician got her a lace handkerchief that she held in her hand.

She also loved lipstick, but for some reason, she would only wear her lipstick right in the middle of both her lips. Lol! So, Claire asked me jokingly if I was going to put her lipstick on like she wore it, and I said, "Nah. Sista is wearing a full coverage on those lips!"

She had never asked me to do her makeup if she passed away, but she did say don't have her looking no kind of way and do not put her face on a t-shirt! So, we didn't have shirts printed with her on them; however, I did make sure her hair was done by one of the best just how she wore it and would have liked it. And I did her make up soft and natural, just the way she would have wanted because she did not wear makeup.

There were over two hundred people in attendance. There was standing room only. Everyone who came to her funeral and/or viewing complimented us on how beautiful she and her entire service was! We went with a nice soft rose/pink color casket with rose gold accents that was accessorized with roses engraved on the casket. Daddy picked out some of the finest rose bouquets and sprays. We all collectively decided to wear the uniform color black to keep it classy, just like Mama.

My mother's pastor preached her eulogy. I wish I could remember what he preached about, but I can't. However, my cousins Jasheika, Sherry, and Moteese all brought the house down in song! We were able to worship with mama one more time and send her off just the way she would have wanted.

There will never be another Dorothy Faye Williams.

Chapter 5
Forgiving the Murderer

Forty-eight hours after the murder of my mama, I was laying in the darkness of midnight, eyes wide open and mind running one million miles a minute. I wish I could tell you that my thoughts were holy, but they weren't! My thoughts were filled with anguish.

I didn't know what was going to happen to my family now. I was afraid my daddy wouldn't make it long after the funeral. I was unsure of how my sister would live her life without giving up. My parents had helped me raise my kids. I was scared for my boys, but I didn't have anything to give them. Every man was for themselves in my household.

I feared for my oldest brother whose son was in the car with my mama, whom she was also helping to raise. I was afraid my niece who was in the car with my mama wouldn't bounce back mentally and emotionally from something so tragic.

Needless to say, I wanted revenge. I did not want God to get it for us! I wanted to get it for my own mama, family, and myself! I was infuriated. I judged whoever this woman was horribly, as one could imagine. When I wanted to kill myself, my kids were the reason I didn't!

How dumb could she be?! I wanted to make her feel the pain she had bestowed on my family and me! She didn't just hurt my mama, but she killed her! She had my niece and nephews laying up in the hospital banged up!

The more I thought about it, the angrier and angrier I grew! There were no more tears in that moment; I was just pissed off! Pure rage! Mind racing and calculating how I was going to make her suffer for what she had done to my mama! To us!

This murderous woman had to pay! And I didn't want to wait on no judge and jurors to tell me and my family what they came up with! No, that just wouldn't be enough! I wanted to catch her slipping. I didn't care who she was with. I wanted to whoop her unmercifully! I felt complete pain and rage!

I was afraid of what the now was going to be for our family without my mama because she was the matriarch and the boss! I was afraid life wasn't going to function without my mama the way it had always been, and it was the lady's fault who killed her! So, she needed to pay!

I could feel the rage in my body. I couldn't lay still. I continued flipping from my right side to my left side. I laid on my back for a minute, looking up toward the ceiling just thinking and thinking.

Finally, I began to apologize to God for what I had planned. Not that I wasn't going to try to go through with these crazy thoughts; I was apologizing because I love Him, and I knew He would want me to do something different than the thoughts I had.

However, I felt out of control in that moment, so I wanted to pre-repent for what I knew I was capable of doing, given the opportunity. I'm so used to talking to God about any and everything that it's automatic, even when I'm at my worst. I wanted God to understand that He wasn't a bad God and that I understood that this had nothing to do with Him and that sometimes as a human being you have different types of emotions and needs that have nothing to do with how He would want you to operate in the Holy Spirit.

Now, this may sound weird or funny to some, but the truth is this is my way of reasoning with

Him when I want to do what I know He doesn't approve of. So, yes, I go to explaining to Him all the things about being a human being that He couldn't possibly understand. I mean, He's God! What would He know, right? (Rolls eyes at myself.)

As I was talking to God about how angry and hurt I was and how irresponsible this woman had to be in order to be so stupid and careless, The Lord never said a word. Instead, He just began to replay certain events in my life that had taken place, that a lot of people didn't even know about, and that over the course of years, I had forgotten about.

I was in a good place in life until this woman killed my mama! I was fasting and praying. I had a brand-new thriving career in the oilfield truck driving. I was single but dating someone who had a little money and knew the Lord for himself. Besides my youngest son cutting up here and there, life was a lot sweeter than it had ever been.

I was seeing growth in my walk with God! My friends were okay, and up to this point, my family was good. It seemed that the struggles of life were finally subsiding, and then this!

As the Lord replayed the past events of my troubled past, one of the events that stood out most was when I was just twenty-two years old, married to a man who was extremely physically, mentally, and emotionally abusive. One day while I was pregnant with my second son, we were driving down the street in north Long Beach. We had just left our apartment, and another argument broke out. I can't remember what the argument was about, but he punched me dead in my mouth, busting my lip. Then he jumped out of the car and began running, so I jumped out of the car in the middle of Paramount Boulevard and started chasing him on foot.

Well, at six months pregnant, I wasn't going to catch him, and I remembered I left my three-year-old son in the car. So, I raced back to my car, jumped in, and drove off, still looking for him in an infuriated state of mind. While in this horrible marriage, I was tricked into believing that I wasn't being abused because, Honey, I fought back every time! And sometimes, if he would get too close to me, I would swing first.

So, this day, instead of just leaving him, like we love to tell people to do when they are in a bad situation with someone they love and are soul tied to or have some type of dependency with their significant other, I did not digress. I drove up the street until I found him crossing over a street called Candlewood. He tried to hurry and run to the bus stop where other pedestrians were standing, but I saw red and hit the gas. It had to have been the Lord who brought me back to my right mind when I hurried and hit the brakes and slightly turned the wheel.

My car did hit the curb, and pedestrians started scattering and running. Thankfully, no one was hurt. If anyone had called the cops, they never came. Well, I didn't stick around to see if they were coming, and my ex had a record, so I'm sure he didn't stick around, either.

Immediately after remembering that event, my heart softened toward the woman who killed my mama. The truth was, I don't know her story, and she had no idea that it was my mama, niece, and nephews in that car. She apparently lost sight of what was most important in that moment, and perhaps, just like me, didn't have the time or wasn't in her right mind to think about the what ifs.

I also realized how much God had done for me! Not to have injured one soul at that bus stop that day, I was immediately grateful and thankful! Then true repentance began to happen. I asked The Lord to forgive me for my thoughts. I told him that if he could just subside the pain a bit so that I may not be so angry. I could truly forgive the way God desired for me to.

The Lord began to let me know that my mom was in no pain. That she was resting with Him. I understand that being with the Lord is the best place we will ever be able to be in; however, my human mind!

The Baby Girl in me wanted my mama here with us! And I still was having trouble with the thought that someone took her from here. I was still having trouble finding it in my heart to forgive the person who did this because although I didn't know a whole lot about her, she and I had something in common, and that was being in domestic violence relationships which is more than likely paired with deep rooted generational curses and ungodly soul-ties. And just like the Lord had forgiven me, I knew it was my responsibility to forgive her. And whenever I would have my day in court with her, it would be my responsibility to let her know that I forgive her, but most importantly, God forgives her.

I laid in my bed crying, repeating, "I forgive her. I forgive her. I forgive her." I had to say it multiple times, and if I'm completely honest, I still have to say it multiple times. I'm learning that depending on the degree and nature of the pain or trauma caused by someone, you will have to choose to forgive that person every time the thought and pain arises.

As a way to vent out my feelings and to somehow keep myself accountable, I went to Facebook and would write my feelings for the moment or that day. So, after this great encounter with God during my time of complete fury, I wrote about how I had forgiven the young lady who killed my mother and how I had planned to show her pictures of my mama.

I wanted to show her that my mama was a human being and that she lived, laughed, loved, cooked, cursed people out, and nurtured us. Lol. She danced. She was funny. She could be a mean girl sometimes, but she always was helping somebody do something. I wanted to give her a sense of what our lives was like before she took my mama's life so she would understand that it wasn't easy to come to this state of forgiveness.

But I also understood that my whole family wasn't on board with forgiveness just yet. They were broken and angry, so their victim impact statement would sound off their true and genuine feelings that they reserved the right to have. But I know my assignment is to forgive, and so I have and will continue to do so.

Secondly, I understand that when you've messed up really bad, someone saying, "You're forgiven" but not expounding may seem like they're just saying what sounds good. So, I want her to know that I can relate to making bad decisions in life, but at some point, I had to leave behind the people who were bringing out the worst in me. With the help of God, I was able to be sustained throughout my healing and deliverance journey. Although she must do time for her crime, I am truly forgiving her.

When I wrote out my thoughts and feelings on Facebook, people rallied around me on social media. They sent messages letting me know that they were now working on forgiving the person who had murdered their loved ones. They were being healed by some of the things that I had written. They knew I loved God and had always uplifted them, but they never knew my love for God was that deep!

The greatest compliments came from my Aunty Wanda who told me that my words were coming from a girl who had evolved into a woman. She was proud of my spiritual growth, and that meant a lot to me. My daddy tells me every time he reads a post how in awe he is with my writings and that I should do something with it. I had no idea writing about my mama's tragic murder would be the first book I'd write, but here we are.

One thing that I've learned throughout my walk with God is that the enemy hates me! As soon as God delivers me, the enemy is there to try to convince me that I'm not delivered. As soon as God heals me, the enemy is there to try to convince my mind that I'm still sick in sin or in my body. As soon as The Lord gets me to see myself in this woman who murdered my mom, the enemy is there trying to get me to focus on the fact that she killed my mama instead of the assignment at hand.

The nice young lady, who happened to be on the scene and was the first person to run to my mama's car after it stopped flipping and slid to a stop, contacted me on Messenger to introduce herself, give her condolences, and to try to give me and my family some closure. Her letter read, "Hello. My name is Jemica. I was the one who climbed in the car to check your mom and to try to get her out. With the help of three guys, we tried to flip the car back over. All I could see was my own mother and didn't want to stop trying to help. But I want to share with you the beautiful face I saw when checking her vitals. I'm a nurse, so I had everything I needed in my car to check her vitals. There was a peace in the middle of all of this chaos that I can't explain. But reading your post, I know it was God. Your mom was full of it and passed that to a complete stranger. I know you're angry at [the woman who killed your mom] in the other vehicle, and I'm not sure if you have heard how this all ended up happening, but she was running from a domestic dispute when this happened. When I went to the window to see if she was alive, the first thing she said was, 'I'm sorry. I don't know their names, but I would like to check on them as well.' And then she mentioned that she was running from a domestic dispute. But I just needed you to know that the light your mother bestowed in you shines through, even in dark times. I lost my dad in an accident almost identical in 2008 on my birthday, and I wish I was able to handle it the way you are. I want you to know I don't know you, but I love you, and there's nothing anyone can do about it. I will continue to pray for your family. Have a blessed night and let me know if there's anything I can do for you."

I know you're probably thinking how sweet of this stranger to reach out to me to give me a sense of peace in the middle of the storm, and I agree! She was so kind, not to only reach out, but she even tried to save my mama's life! How can I ever repay her generosity?! However, sometime just before she sent this beautiful letter, we had gotten word that the young lady who killed my mother was not really running from being harmed and that she had run herself and children into a tree in an incident before this. She had a history of attempting suicide/homicide, and my family became one of her victims during one of her suicide attempts. She wasn't even drunk at the time like previous reports had been saying; she was solely under the influence of demons when she killed my mama.

My response to this sweet lady was, "Thank you! Thank you! Thank you! Unfortunately, the lady lied to you… she actually ran into a tree in a prior incident months before this happened, trying to deliberately kill herself and her children… her husband showed up on the scene and was angry with the police because he tried to tell them before this happened that she is mental… they ignored him… you have no idea how much this means to my family and I."

Her response was, "Thank you so much. I hope she gets the help she needs."

In that moment, the enemy tried to steal my peace and the forgiveness I told God and everyone who read my posts that I was to give this murderous woman! How dare the lady who tried to save my mama's life feel bad for the woman who killed my mama?!

I felt the anger all over again, so I responded, "Yeah, I guess that's the least that can happen since my mama is dead! Thanks again so much."

I remember putting my phone down. I needed to get away from everyone, so I went into my parents' hallway bathroom, got down on my knees, and cried out to God, "Please, God, help me! I can't do it! Please, God, it's only been three days. If they haven't started cutting on my mama and removing her blood, you can work a miracle! We won't be scared of her; we will just be happy to have her back! Please!"

The Lord didn't speak back in the moment, so I got up off my knees, washed my face, and went back into the den with everyone else. I sat quietly for a few moments before letting everyone know that the lady who tried to save Mama had contacted me. I can't remember if I read what she said or just told them what she said happened. But, like me, as soon as I got to the part that said she hoped the woman who killed Mama got the help she needed, my entire family was turned off!

I spent the next few days preparing to say my final goodbyes to my mama and trying to remain saved and keep my sanity. I thought forgiveness was all that God required of me. But I would later learn that He wanted me to do more than forgive the woman who seemingly so carelessly took my mama's life. He wanted to give me more insight over the course of time. This would result in Him giving me His reasoning for allowing it to be my mom that night and not any one of the other three cars that preceded her on that road.

As one could imagine, the death of my mama replayed in my head so many times. Although I knew she couldn't hear me, I would ask Mama, "Did you feel it? Are you really okay? Can you please come talk to Dayday? Will you visit Daddy and comfort him? Is heaven more than we could ever imagine?"

I didn't have the guts to look at the autopsy report, although I wanted to know what killed Super Woman! The reality of what was done to my mama may keep me from being able to forgive wholeheartedly, so to this day, I have not read the report. I made a declaration when my mama was murdered, "The devil is in trouble now!" And I meant every word of it!

Just six months prior to my mama being murdered, I was hit by some Caucasian kids who were traveling at high speeds. Lucky for me, I was in my tanker truck, so I wasn't harmed. It was apparent to me that the enemy waged war on my family! And I wasn't going to stand for it!

I understood that I could not curse the devil out to win this war, neither could I physically beat him down. I understood that the only way I could win was by way of the Holy Spirit, and I was down for the fight! I also declared that I would win more souls for Christ than I could have ever thought possible! I knew I had to conquer forgiveness in order for this battle to be won the correct way! And I was all for it! I just needed to get around the pain, which was turning into depression.

Although I heard the people telling me how proud they were of me and how strong they thought I was or how much I was really helping them on social media, it wasn't equivalent to the life of my mama! It felt like I should be preaching on mountain tops, standing on corners with microphones declaring the word of the Lord! It felt like something more needed to be done to vindicate my mama!

What does one do when they are trying with all their strength to remain holy and in relationship with God, while the human side of them is battling so profusely? I would lay in bed and not be able to move for three days at a time. I was trying not to cry so uncontrollably that it would alarm my sons. I wanted to be okay. I wanted to be my normal self again.

Depression was triumphing over this mission to forgive and let live. I was a total wreck! But who was I going to tell? My entire family was affected by this, and all of us were just trying to make it. God was literally all I had.

I remember going to God, asking so many questions. The whys. The Is-He-sure-this-didn't-catch-Him-off-guard? The Am-I-honestly-going-to-make-it-through-this? Also pleading with God not to take anyone else in our family no time soon because it was way too hard!

I would cry out, "God, I want to forgive her, but she killed my mama! How am I supposed to really do this?"

All for Him to respond, "You have to give it to Me." And other times He'd say, "Will you get up and worship?"

I was weak. Literally weak. I would stand on the side of my bed and try to extend my hands to worship. I couldn't shout like I wanted to, so I would turn on worship music and try to tap in, but the church music made me think of Mama.

Finally on day three of one of my depression spurts, I got up, and I just began to pray in tongues. It was the only form of worship or prayer that I could muscle up. Something broke! I just started crying and worshiping, and I could hear the Holy Spirit saying, "There it goes."

I realized that it wasn't that I was taking my forgiveness back; it was just that the pain was so heavy, I couldn't operate in anything outside of depression and despair. But finally, I seemed better after my breakthrough. Only to realize that it was temporary. I would have to press on daily like never before!

Chapter 6
The Perfect Introduction

3:33 am prayer has been my assignment for years. Fasting and praying has been a lifestyle for me for quite some time, but none of those things came easy to me anymore. So, if I wanted freedom, if I wanted to be able to stand in my God-given authority again, I had to fight! I needed people who could fight with and for me! And I was desperate enough to reach out for help.

My sister in Christ, Makayla, had just lost her son a few weeks prior to my mama passing. We were both barely making it some days and holding strong others. The church she attended at the time was having a prophetic healing and deliverance service, and she invited me, so I took her up on her offer!

When I went to the service, it had been about four months since Mama had been promoted to glory. It was four months too long! I needed God in a way I had never experienced Him because I was going through something horribly that I had never experienced before. I'm so glad that I serve a God who shows up right on time!

When we walked into the service, I immediately felt the presence of God! But it would take a few hours before I would get my release! The guest prophet was to bring the Word on the second half of the service. This was one of those old school shut-ins, except it was in the daytime.

During service, I was able to close my eyes and just enjoy service and being in the presence of the Holy Spirit because I hadn't been able to tap in like I normally would. My friends and those who know me would tell you that I don't need a church building or church music to worship! But this season was different. I was depleted, and I needed Holy Ghost emergency assistance!

At last, it was the second part of the service. The prophet whom I had never seen before a day in my life stood up and began to sing some prophetic melody. He began to release Word over the house, and people were crying and shouting and falling out. But I could only shed a few tears here and there with my hands extended.

So as the people of God began to scream out, shout, and be slain in the spirit, I did only what I knew to do. I began assisting the aisle workers with moving chairs so the people could shout freely, making sure no one around me hit the ground, and passing out tissue paper. The church was on fire! The man of God was prophesying to people like he knew them personally! It was amazing!

At some point, everyone in the church was either slain in the spirit or at the alter crying. But I was sitting over to the side in the back of the small storefront church silently when the prophet looked up at me and said, "Come here."

I walked up to the front of the church with my hands extended, not sure of what he would say to me, but ready for whatever. He read the pages of the last four months of my life as if I had it plastered on my shirt in bold print letters.

He looked at me and said, "Oh, you're something else in the spirit, too." Then he backed away from me and said, "Whew, but your mouth still needs deliverance." I smiled slightly, and then he said, "Oh, am I talking to the wrong person?"

I laughed and said, "Nah, you're right!"

He began singing that prophetic song without words again, and then he turned to me and said, "The Lord shows me depression."

I immediately began to weep.

"Oh, I see," the prophet said, in agreeance with what the Lord was telling him. "Ohhh, I get it. Yeah, I felt the same way earlier this year when my grandmother passed away suddenly."

I buckled! I began to cry so hard I couldn't breathe.

Then the prophet hollered out, "God, how am I supposed to live without my mama?!"

And I lost it! I let out a scream I have never heard come from me before. I kicked my feet like a little girl throwing a tantrum. I rolled around those people's church like I was a long-term member and felt no embarrassment! I was trying to catch my breath, but I couldn't. I heard Prophet tell the people, "She's alright, she's alright. Let her alone."

I must have cried on the floor for ten to fifteen minutes before I was able to pull it together. I hadn't even cried that hard at my mama's funeral! Finally, I was able to stand up.

The prophet asked me to come to him again as he was going to wash my hands. He said, "Look at me. Now breathe! You haven't been able to breathe since all of this happened! Oh, I see. It's the way it happened!"

And I cried out some more! Everything that I had been saying to God or thinking and not saying at all, the prophet showed up and spoke it for me!

Prophet then looked at me and said, "You're going to be alright. Mother is okay now." He wrapped his shawl around me and said, "This is how the Lord is wrapping you in his arms."

He assured me that I would be able to run on. Then he washed and anointed my hands.

My life hasn't been the same since. God used the prophet to help break depression completely off of me, and I went right back into effective 3:33 am prayer, worshipping and prophesying whenever the Lord wants to use me.

I thanked the Lord and told him, "Now, I'm ready to get back to doing the work!"

However, I still had questions surrounding my mother's traumatic exit from earth to glory. Why did she have to go out that way? But I was also able to see how God answered her prayers. Mama did not want to ever be so sick that she couldn't take care of herself or wipe her own tail. So, although the crash was harsh, it was quick, and she didn't suffer.

Mama would have never been able to live anyway had something happened to one of her grandchildren or the children in the car of the woman who killed her. The oldest daughter of the woman who killed my mama was ejected from the car. She survived, but there were some injuries. And the woman's baby girl suffered severe brain damage from the wreck, and for the longest time, the doctors didn't think that she was going to make it. I thanked God for sparing Mama that level of trauma, regret, and depression that wouldn't have allowed her to move forward in her life. I was so grateful just to be able to breathe and worship again, and now it was time to give the enemy a run for his money!

One day, I was missing Mama, and I was having a moment. I've learned that even though I received a major breakthrough, and I'm able to function again, that doesn't mean that missing Mama won't still hurt, and that sometimes I still want God to explain to me the happenings! I've heard the story over and over again of what happened to my mom and why the woman did what she did, but sometimes, it just seems like there has got to be more! Even if there isn't. The truth is the woman was riddled with demonic influences. Period.

The Lord sometimes asked me questions in order to cause me to think, just for Him to answer the questions that He's asked me. The Lord asked me, "What if the persons in the vehicles who preceded your mother weren't saved? Do you know that I created time? And that I am the only One aware of the time life is birthed into this world and when it will end on earth and begin in eternity?"

Then the Lord gave me this vision of a huge angel covering my niece Sabrina who was in the front seat next to my Mama, and simultaneously snatching Mama up quickly! I understood that vision very well. It was actually an answer to one of my many questions of how? The officer himself said it was a miracle that Sabrina not only lived but walked away without injury. She was never knocked out during the occurrence and could recall everything that happened.

Finally, the Lord asked, "What if the family members of the people in the cars that preceded your mother on that road weren't saved? Who would be there to introduce your mother's murderer to me?"

I sat and wept. I understood the task that had been placed in my lap. God placed the task upon me to introduce my mama's murderer to Him. I never really saw my mother as a sacrifice until a few people mentioned it, including my sister, but now it is clear to me. God trusted me to introduce the murderer to Him! She killed my mama to meet me so that I could introduce her to HIM.

It wasn't anyone else's time to go. Perhaps, the family members of the people who preceded my Mama weren't saved or spiritually mature enough to forgive someone for murdering their loved one, let alone offering them Christ. We were chosen for this by God, and to be perfectly honest, it only makes sense for the woman who killed my mother to finally meet Jesus! The one who saves, delivers, forgives, and restores.

Although I am totally persuaded that God knows all things and that He does all things well! I will also admit that I thought this was over the top for an introduction until I was reminded of the life of Jesus and how dramatic many of His interactions with people were. Even when there was no audience, by the time the Lord finished working the miracles, the people would be so happy that they'd run and tell others all about Him!

Take for instance the woman from Samaria who met Jesus at the well of Jacob in John chapter four. I can hear her now, running back to tell the people how she met a man. "Could he be the Messiah?" she exclaimed, while urging them to come see Him! In which they did. He ministered, and they asked him to stay. He stayed for two days, feeding their souls, and they, too, became believers!

My attention is also brought to Acts chapter nine. This is the story of Saul, whose name was later changed to Paul, who hated Jesus and Christians. But on his way to Damascus with others who traveled with him to arrest and kill believers, he was encountered by a bright light, which blinded him. He was also encountered by the voice of The Most High who confronted him, asking, "Saul, why do you persecute me?" This conversation would only lead Saul to be commissioned to continue his route to Damascus where he would receive his orders from the Lord on what to do next—meet Ananias who would lay hands on him. Saul received the Holy Spirit, was baptized and received by disciples, as well as received his sight, which had been taken from him on the road. He began sharing the gospel of Jesus Christ and received a name change to Paul.

Ther are so many more dramatic encounters, or perfect introductions to Jesus, if you will. Both scriptural and from personal testimonies that I have had the privilege to hear. As I realize that though it's my personal journey, it is no different than other believers who have, too, had to face enormous challenges and still be a beacon of light to ensure that before the Messiah returns, everyone will have had the opportunity to meet Christ.

Now it is with pure gladness that I have accepted the commission to one day face the woman who was so downtrodden that she attempted suicide and murdered my Mama in the act. Not to beat her over the head with what she has done. Not to persecute any more than the judge and jurors. But instead to introduce her to the one and only Messiah, who died so that she may have life and live life more abundantly.

As tears, not of sorrow, roll down my face, I accept that though we miss Mama greatly and more than words can ever convey, the end of her life here on earth was worth the sacrifice. She now rests in His bosom, so that someone could have the "perfect introduction to Jesus Christ".

Encouragement

When the enemy hits you with his best shot, although you may be wounded to your very core, you fight with everything you have left! A'Nesu Williams encourages you to fight back with an offering of praise and genuine worship to our Lord and Savior Jesus Christ! And if you find that you don't have the words in your native tongue, then utilize your Holy Language! Let the Holy Spirit make utterances for you! Romans 8:26 says that The Holy Spirit helps us in our weakness. We don't know what we ought to pray for. But the Holy Spirit prays for us with groanings that cannot be expressed in words. If for any reason at all you are unable to open your mouth at all, then with whatever strength you have left, lift your hands before God! Even the raising of our hands is a sign of worship! A gesture of surrender, adoration, and praise!

When I was younger, I watched wrestling, and there would be times that there was a tag team event. If one wrestler on the team was being beaten up, if he could just muster up the strength to stretch his arms out far enough for his teammate to touch him, then his help would enter the ring! I come to tell you, Brothers and Sisters, that the enemy is always going to play dirty! But the good news is that he's fighting a losing battle because he cannot defeat God! And when we choose to worship, even at our lowest, it compels God to show up on our behalf! Lift your hands to the Lord in worship, and watch HIM tag HIMSELF IN!

MY FINAL THOUGHTS

The purpose of writing this book is to show people that we can overcome anything through Christ Jesus! Perhaps, someone has been dealing with grief for a while, and they would like to overcome it, but don't know how. I'm hoping this book encourages them to get with God so they may be healed and delivered from the bondage of grief and bitterness.

I want people to know that we can't miss the assignment, even when tragedy strikes. I want to make it clear that we are still responsible to get the assignment done. We can, with the help of God, forgive what people would deem unforgivable! We have to stop being upset with God because death happens. We all have to die, and sometimes it comes by way of tragic events. Either way, we should understand that God doesn't make mistakes. The death of a loved one didn't catch the Lord by surprise. He's still in control.

God does all things well. It was obviously my mom's time to go. It was obviously time for the woman who killed my mother to meet the one who will heal and deliver her from the demons that have plagued her life! So, what looks like and is a tragedy in the natural is a win-win in the kingdom of God! My mother was welcomed into heaven, and the woman who killed my mother has the opportunity to meet Jesus and get delivered.

Meet the Author

A'Nesu Williams is the founder of Worship While We Wait LLC (WWWW, LLC), where she encourages women to continue to worship and serve while they're waiting on a move of God! She hosts a unique Bible study called "Gospel Gossip" every Thursday evening at 7 pm CST where she breaks down the Bible in such a way that even 5-year-olds can
understand. A'Nesu believes that the Lord gifted her with an ability to teach in this way because of her and one her son's neurodivergent way of learning. She went to God with sincere concerns that no matter what age or background the women God would have her to encounter, they would be able to receive from her exactly what God's Word is conveying.

A'Nesu is the fourth of five children and the youngest girl of her parents' children. She was born and raised in Long Beach, California to Clifford and Dorothy Williams, Jr. She attended the St. Luke Holy Missionary Baptist Church with her family where Pastor Maurice Revell Nelson, Sr. was their pastor. She accepted Christ at an early age; however, she took the scenic route to her close-knit relationship with God!

She is a daughter, a mother, a sister, a friend, a stylist by trade, and a truck driver by trade. But most importantly, she is the daughter of The Most High King.

Thank you for reading! Please leave a review wherever reviews are accepted. God bless you, God keep you, may He make His face shine upon you.

Made in the USA
Coppell, TX
07 January 2026